Best 1

oJ
The Colophon Cafe
Fairhaven, Washington

*A Stirring Plot for Cooking Pots, starring
Quality, Service, Consistency, and Cleanliness!*

Mama Colophon

Published by
Mama Colophon, Inc.
1208 11th St. (Fairhaven)
Bellingham, Washington, 98225
360-647-0092
*For more recipes and information, log on to
<www.colophoncafe.com>*

The who, what, when, where and why of Fairhaven

In 1858, because of the gold strikes in British Columbia, Fort Bellingham, located on what was then Whatcom Bay, found itself the center of about 15,000 people, and the Bay was clogged with ships.

During that manic time, Whatcom Bay was the most convenient port to get goods from the U.S. to Canada's Fort Langley and the Fraser River.

In 1883, a man named Dan Harris, having made his own gold strike by selling rice, vegetables, hardware and hard liquor out of a sloop in Whatcom Bay, bought a claim south of the towns of Whatcom and Bellingham.

Hoping to attract eastern investors, Harris named his claim Fairhaven, built a hotel and began to offer lots for gold. By 1885 he had done well enough to move to Los Angeles!

The real-estate boom of 1888 and 1889 brought Nelson Bennet, a wealthy developer to the area. He brought railroads into town, connecting Fairhaven with Whatcom to the north and with the main line between Vancouver, B.C. and Vancouver, Wash.

Another Californian, Jim Wardner, organized the Fairhaven Water Works Co., the Fairhaven Electric Light Co., the Samish Lake Logging & Milling Co., the Cascade Club and two banks. His 23-room "mansion," Wardner's Castle, is on the historical register.

The Depression of 1893 ended the Fairhaven boom. But coal mines, timber and shipping kept the towns of Whatcom and Fairhaven (which included the old town of Bellingham) going, and in 1904 they merged into a single city, Bellingham.

Taken from Paul Dorpat's "Now and Then," and from the Whatcom County Centennial Committee.

What does it all mean?

COLOPHON: (kol'e fon')

1. A publishers distinctive emblem.

2. An inscription at the end of a book, usually with facts relative to its publication.

3. Greek koloph'on: summit, finishing touch, the last word.

4. The Colophon Cafe is the last word in good eating.

5. Pronounced "Call-a-fawn" Cafe

Mama Colophon

Contents

Dressing & Salads

Desserts, etc.

Alphabetical Index on page 70.

Mama Colophon

"When you know a thing, to hold that
you know it; and when you do not
know a thing, to allow that you do not
know it – this is knowledge."
... Confucius

Savory Soups

"Ancient drums echoed eerily through the lush green jungle as a scantily-clad Tarzan carefully stirred the thick soup in his tree-house kitchen, hoping fervently that Jane would swoon over his culinary efforts and melt into his arms in an uncontrollable passion."

From: "Tarzan and the Magic Ginger Root," by Mama Colophon

Mama Colophon

The *Original* African Peanut Soup

*This often-copied-never-duplicated recipe was created in the fall of 1985
Ginger root, chilies and garlic give it a distinctive, spicy taste
which some people call addictive!
It has been featured in Barbara Williams' "Coasting & Cooking Cookbook",
along with recipes from the finest restaurants on the Washington Coast.*

Blend in food processor:	1 oz. fresh ginger root, scrubbed and chunked 2 cloves garlic 1 tsp. crushed chili peppers
Add to processor and chop, leaving chunky, then add to soup pot.	3-1/4 cups canned or fresh diced tomatoes 1-3/4 cups dry roasted unsalted peanuts 1 medium onion, chopped
Add and cook to 165°:	1-1/2 cups chicken stock 3 cups water
Make a Roux paste. Add to thicken:	1/4 cup flour mixed into 1/4 cup melted butter
Finally, add:	2-4 cups diced tomatoes, canned or fresh 1/2 lb. cooked and cubed turkey or chicken

*Whisk warm Roux into soup and simmer to thicken.
Heat to 160°. Add final tomatoes to thin and
to add chunkiness to soup. Reduce heat to 145° to serve.
For vegetarian version, leave out the turkey or chicken,
and use vegetable stock instead of chicken stock.
Garnish with peanuts. Serves 6-8.*

As the fog crept across the grey winter
harbor, Captain Vancouver peered out
at the heavily forested coastline, exclaiming,
"Thick as pea soup, this blasted weather!"
Then went below for a pint.

From "the History of Fairhaven"
by Mama Colophon

Split Pea Soup

*Our simple, healthy version is vegetarian
and low-fat . . . and thick as fog!
We garnish it with our own homemade croutons.*

Lightly sauté in a little butter:	1 cup finely diced yellow onion
Bring to boil. Cook covered on simmer for 1 to 1 1/2 hours, or until carrots are done:	5 cups water 1 lb. green split peas, rinsed 1 medium diced carrot Salt & pepper to taste

*Thin with hot water if needed, but it
should be as thick as fog!
Garnish with Colophon Croutons.
Serves 4-6*

Colophon Croutons

*The Colophon's own toasted garlic croutons are great on
split pea soup as a garnish, or tossed in a Caesar salad!*

Cut enough day old bread to cover a cookie sheet.
Mix together 1/2 cup melted butter with
1 tsp. each of garlic, thyme, parsley and tarragon
Drizzle mixture over bread, stirring as you go.
Put in 400° oven for 8 minutes.
Stir well.
Put back in for 3 to 4 minutes
until they are golden toasty brown.
Leave out to cool.
Store in sealed containers.

"Zapata leapt swiftly from the horse,
stormed into the hacienda,
and after having been gone
six long weeks, strode, not to kiss
his waiting wife, but to the kitchen
for a hearty bowl of soup."

From "Passions of Zapata"
by Mama Colophon

Yum!

Mexican Corn & Bean Sopa

One of the most popular soups ever to come from the Colophon, the Mexican corn & Bean Sopa has been featured in many publications since we created it. It's vegetarian, low in fat and delicious.

Sauté in a little olive oil:
- 1 medium finely diced onion
- 3 cloves minced garlic

Add to soup pot and heat to a slow boil:
- 1 (15 oz.) can diced tomatoes or equal amount of chopped fresh tomatoes and tomato juice.
- 2 (15 oz.) cans red kidney beans, drained
- 1 (24 oz.) can vegetable juice

In a small bowl mix, then add hot water to a paste-like consistency, Add to pot and heat:
- 3 tsp. chili powder
- 1 tsp. sugar
- 1 tsp. cumin
- 1/2 tsp. black pepper

Add to pot, and heat to 160° Simmer for 1 to 2 hours.
- 1 (1 lb.) bag frozen corn kernels

Thin with water or vegetable juice. Garnish with blue and yellow Tortilla Chips Serves 6-8

Tomato Parmesan Soup

Friday is always tomato soup day at the Colophon. This Italian flavor soup is easy to make and excellent any day of the week!

In a soup pot, sauté in 1 tbsp. butter or olive oil until tender:
- 1/2 onion, chopped
- 1/4 cup chopped parsley
- 2 cloves minced garlic

Add and heat to 160°:
- 2 (15 oz.) cans tomato soup
- 1 can water
- 1 (15 oz.) canned diced tomatoes, or equal amount of fresh diced tomatoes
- 1/2 tsp. black pepper
- 1 tsp. thyme

Garnish with shredded Parmesan cheese or a sprig of parsley
Serves 4-6.

Variation: If you prefer cheddar cheese, add 1/4 cup of sherry and 1 cup chopped cheddar cheese to the soup mixture, and warm to 160°. Garnish with cheddar wedge instead of grated parmesan.

Cream of Broccoli Soup

A rich and creamy winter's day soup created by the Colophon to make everyone a broccoli fan!

Sauté in soup pot:	1 tbsp. butter 1 medium onion, minced 3 cloves garlic, minced
Add, cover with water, and cook:	3/4 lb. thawed frozen broccoli, chopped
Reduce heat and add:	2 stalks celery, chopped 1/2 tsp. salt 1/2 tsp. pepper Squeeze of lemon Dash of Tabasco
In separate bowl, combine and whip until smooth, then add to soup pot and heat to 160 degrees:	1/4 lb softened cream cheese 1 cup warmed milk
At 160 degrees, add:	Roux: 3 tbsp. flour mixed into 3 tbsp. melted butter

Reduce heat to 145° and thin with milk.

*Garnish with cheddar cheese wedge
or broccoli crowns.
Serves 8-10*

Broccoli Cheddar Chowder

"It is well known that the cow is a sacred being,"
Ghandi said, "but this cheddar soup does inspire one
to respect it even more."

Sauté onions & garlic in butter. Put in soup pot:
- 1-1/2 medium onion, chopped
- 1 garlic clove, minced

In soup pot, cook potatoes, broccoli and red peppers, covered in water until tender:
- 3/4 lb. chopped broccoli
- 3/4 lb. chopped potatoes
- 1-1/2 red pepper, chopped
- 3 tbsp. butter

When vegetables are cooked through, add cumin, salt, pepper, dry mustard and flour:
- 1-1/2 tsp. cumin
- 1-1/2 tsp. salt
- 1/4 tsp. black pepper
- 3/4 tsp. dry mustard
- 3 tbsp. all purpose flour

Add cream and cheese until cheese is melted:
- 1 cup heavy cream
- 2 cups grated cheddar cheese

Serve garnished with shredded cheddar.
Serves 4-6.

Manhattan Clam Chowder

For years the Colophon served only a white clam chowder, until we tasted this wonderful red version created by our soup chef. It's spicy, delicious and easy to make.

In soup pot, cook until potatoes are done, in just enough water to cover:

Happy as a clam!

1 diced med. white onion
3 small cubed potatoes
1 peeled, diced carrot
Juice from 2 (6-1/2 oz.) cans chopped clams
1 (8 oz.) bottle clam juice
2 tbsp. parsley
1 diced red pepper
2 tbsp. instant mashed potatoes
1 tsp. thyme
Salt & pepper to taste

Add, heat to slow boil, then turn down to simmer for 10 minutes or so before serving.

1 (14-1/2 oz.) can diced tomatoes with juice
2 cups vegetable juice
2 cans of chopped clams (that were left from the juice you put in)

Garnish with goldfish crackers.
Serves 4-6

Dancing clams are fine for the big city, but have you seem our hoofing holsteins?

"Gazpacho!" He declared as his partner
sneezed. His friend remembered after
that to hold his breath while opening
the black pepper.

Gazpacho

A spicy, cold tomato soup, full of healthy veggies.
Excellent for a summer meal.

Mix together the day before serving in a large bowl and chill overnight:

3 (15 oz.) cans diced tomatoes, or fresh tomatoes that have been peeled and chopped
46 oz. vegetable juice cocktail
1/4 cup white onion, chopped
3 cucumbers, peeled, seeded and diced
1/2 bunch celery, diced
1/4 bunch cilantro, minced
1 bunch green onions, chopped
2 tbsp. olive oil
2 tbsp. garlic, minced
A good dash of Tabasco
1 tsp. salt
1 tsp. pepper

Thin with chilled vegetable juice if too thick.
Chill pot and bowls in freezer before serving.
For added flavor, serve with small shrimp
and a dollop of sour cream on top.
Garnish with tortilla chips.

Serves 6-8

Curried Corn & Cheddar Chowder

The second place winner at the
1986 Chowder Cook Off in Bellingham

Whip together in soup pot:	1 qt. hot water 6 oz. softened cream cheese
Add & heat to a slow boil:	1 (16 oz.) can creamed corn 4 tsp. curry powder 1 tsp. black pepper 1/2 cup chopped onion
Add & heat to a slow boil:	1-1/2 lbs. frozen corn kernels 2 stalks celery, chopped
Add, reduce heat to a simmer:	Roux—3 tbsp. flour mixed into 3 tbsp. melted butter
Stir gently into soup:	1 cup cubed & floured cheddar cheese, tossed and shaken in a bag with 2 tbsp. flour

Garnish with cheddar cheese,
grated or cut into shapes.
Serves 6-8

Thai Ginger Chicken Soup

*This extraordinary, exotic soup won the
1995 Allied Arts Soup Festival in Bellingham.*

Cook until rice is done:
- 2-1/2 cups chicken broth
- 1 cup rice

Add to soup pot, cook until temperature reaches 160 degrees:
- 1 tbsp. "Taste of Thai" Green Curry Base⁺
- 1 tbsp. garlic powder
- 2 tsp. thyme
- 2 tsp. basil
- 1 tbsp. fresh ground ginger root
- 1 lb. cooked chicken, chopped

Turn heat down slightly and add:
- 1 (14 oz.) can coconut milk
- Dash of lime juice
- Dash of lemon juice

Serve at 150 degrees. Thin with water if desired. Rice will make mixture very thick.

⁺ *Curry base contains: chilies, onion, garlic galanga, lemon kaffir, and lime peel.
We sell it at the Colophon if you can't find it.*

*Garnish with fresh parsley.
Serves 4-6.*

Pollo Tortilla Soupa

*The idea for this unique soup was borrowed
from a street vendor in La Paz, Mexico.*

Sauté onion and garlic in hot oil until onion is tender. Add chicken cook about 5 minutes:	2 tbsp. oil 1 medium onion (diced) 5 cloves garlic (minced) 1/2 lb. chicken (cooked, cubed)
Blend until liquid in food processor, add to pot:	2 (1 lb.) cans tomatoes
Add broth and spices, heat to 160°:	6 cups chicken broth 2 tsp. oregano 1 tsp. cumin 1 tsp. marjoram 1 tsp. thyme 1 tsp. black pepper 1 tsp. salt
For serving:	Mozzarella cheese (shredded) Sour cream Avocado & tortilla chips

*To serve, fill soup bowl 1/2 full with broken (not
crushed) tortilla chips, cover chips with shredded
mozzarella cheese, fill with hot soup.*

*Garnish with sour cream and/or avocado
and whole tortilla chips.
Serves 6-8*

Salmon Dill Bisque

*By popular demand, a rich and creamy
Northwest favorite!*

Combine and puree in
food processor:

1 carrot, medium
1 red pepper, small
1 green pepper, small
1/2 onion, small
1 celery stalk, diced

Add spices, cover with
water and cook until done:

1 tsp. garlic, granulated
1 tsp. dill weed
3/4 tsp. pepper
2 tbsp. lemon juice

Whisk in Roux to thicken:

Roux: mix 3 tbsp. melted
   butter with 3 tbsp. flour

Turn down slightly
and add:

8 oz. smoked salmon,
   deboned and chopped
   in food processor

Thin as desired with:

1 pint Half & Half

*May be garnished with
a dash of dill weed
or a fresh sprig of dill.
Serves 6-8*

A Swishy Wishy?

A cow is a completely automatic milk-manufacturing machine. It is encased in untanned leather and mounted on four vertical, movable supports, one on each corner.

The front end contains the cutting and grinding mechanism, as well as the headlights, air inlet and exhaust, a bumper and a foghorn.

At the rear is the dispensing apparatus and an automatic fly swatter.

The central portion houses a hydrochemical conversion plant. This consists of four fermentation and storage tanks connected in series by an intricate network of flexible plumbing.

This section also contains the heating plant complete with automatic temperature controls, pumping station and main ventilating system.

The waste-disposal apparatus is located at the rear of this central section.

In brief, the externally visual features are:
two lookers, two hookers, four stander-uppers,
four hanger-downers and a swishy wishy.

Dutch Tomato Gouda

*This cheesy tomato soup is really a
"gouda" Dutch treat!*

Sauté onions in a pan: 1 cup onions, diced

Add to soup pot and
combine with tomatoes,
vegetable juice, water,
vegetable base and spices:

11 oz. diced tomatoes,
undrained
15 oz. vegetable juice
1 2/3 cup water
2 tsp. vegetable base
1/3 tsp. thyme
2/3 tsp. oregano
1/3 tsp. salt
1/3 tsp. black pepper

Purée one cup of soup
and return to pot.
Add sugar, and let dissolve:

5 tbsp. sugar

Then add grated Gouda and
Half & Half. Heat to 160°.

1/3 lb. Gouda cheese, grated
2/3 cup Half & Half

Garnish with grated Gouda or parsley.
Serves 4-6.

Roasted Red Pepper
Cheddar Soup

Another great cheesy soup, but without the tomatoes!

Sauté onions in olive oil. Transfer to soup pot.	1 cup chopped onion 2 tbsp. olive oil
In soup pot, cook onions and potatoes until potatoes are tender:	1/2 lb. baking potato, chopped
Purée cooked potato mixture, along with roasted peppers, then return to soup pot:	2 large red peppers, roasted & chopped
Add heated milk, Worcestershire, Tabasco and grated Cheddar Stir until cheese is melted.	2 cups milk, steamed or heated 1 tsp. Worcestershire sauce Tabasco to taste 14 oz. grated Cheddar cheese

Garnish with cilantro sprigs.
Serves 4-6.

Spicy Moroccan Bean

This is one of those exotic soups that everyone wants to try. It's a bit spicy, so be cautious with the pepper, although the milk helps tone it down a bit.

In soup pot, cook onions and vegetable base until onions are translucent.

1-1/2 cups chopped onion
1-1/4 tsp. vegetable base

Add potatoes and beans, cover with water, and cook thoroughly.

3 oz. red kidney beans, drained
1-1/2 cups chopped potatoes

Once potatoes are tender, add spices, soy sauce, milk and potato flakes.

1/8 tsp. black pepper
1/8 tsp. white pepper
1/8 tsp. cayenne pepper
2 tsp. curry powder
1/3 cup soy sauce
2/3 cup steamed milk
1 tbsp. potato flakes

*To add thickness, purée about 1/2 of the soup mixture.
Heat to 160°.
Garnish with sour cream. Serves 4-6.*

The diner is an American institution. It was started in 1872 by an enterprising peddler with a cart. These lunch carts became walk-in wagons where people could sit down, and were popular all over the Northeast . . . so popular and numerous that laws were passed banning them. By 1912, the wagons were turned into permanent structures and the 24-hour diner was born.

Diners were so popular they gradually moved west, and eventually even to Fairhaven. Now we have cafes and drive-ins and espresso stands, but no diners.

There was a certain lingo that servers shouted when placing orders, that evolved out of the diner era.

- Frog sticks! (french fries)
- Nervous pudding! (jello)
- Splash of red noise! (tomato soup)
- Mud! (chocolate ice cream)
- Radio sandwich! (tuna)
- Houseboat! (banana split)
- City juice! (glass of water)
- Baby! (glass of milk)
- Hold the hail! (no ice)
- Sinkers and suds! (donuts and coffee)
- Squeeze one! (orange juice)
- Bossy in a bowl (beef stew)
- Wrecked hen fruit! (scrambled egg)
- Pair of drawers! (coffee)
- On wheels! (to go)
- Bum the British! (toasted English muffin)

And then there is that well loved remark made by an irate waiter . . . You Shoulda Had It Toasted!

Sweet Potato Bisque

This bisque is nutty, but good. It would be great for the holidays

---

Sauté butter, onion, leeks, garlic, bay leaf and carrots until veggies are tender:

1 cup chopped onion
3/4 cup chopped leek
1 med. clove garlic, minced
1 cup chopped carrots
1-3/4 tbsp. butter
1 bay leaf

Add sweet potatoes and baking potatoes, vegetable base and water. Cook thoroughly. Discard bay leaf. Purée mixture carefully in a food processor and return to pot. Add white wine and heat to 160°.

1-1/2 lbs. sweet potatoes, diced
1/2 lb. baking potato, diced
1 tsp. vegetable base
3/4 cup dry white wine
1 cup water

Spread pecans evenly on baking sheet. In a bowl, mix melted butter, brown sugar and paprika. Drizzle over pecans, mix and bake for about 10 minutes at 350°.

1 cup pecans
1-1/2 tbsp. butter, melted
1 tsp. brown sugar
Pinch of paprika

Garnish soup with the pecans.

Jack Spratt would eat no fat.
His wife would eat no lean.
And so between the two, you see,
. . . she finally sued for divorce
and with her alimony was able to
buy and eat all the fat she wanted
without having to listen to Jack's
complaints.

Mama Colophon

Popular
Favorites

"Most definitely a thumbs up kind of
chili," he announced confidently.
"And don't even think about putting any
cow in it."

*From "Get Those Reviewers Out
of My Kitchen!"
by Mama Colophon*

Mama Colophon

Ray's Turkey Chili

*An amazing chili
made without beef or beans!*

Heat oil in a large soup pot and add these, stirring until cooked:	3 tbsp. vegetable or olive oil 1 chopped red onion 1 chopped yellow onion 2 chopped leeks 6 chopped garlic cloves
Mix these together, adding just enough of the beer to form a thin paste. Stir paste into cooked vegetables:	2 tbsp. flour 4-6 tbsp. chili powder 1 tbsp. oregano 1 tbsp. salt 2 tbsp. cumin powder 1 to 2 tsp. cayenne pepper Bottle of cold beer
Add and stir well:	3 lbs. cooked chopped turkey breast 2 (14 1/2 oz.) cans stewed tomatoes (with juice) 1 (14 oz.) can tomato sauce 4-5 tbsp. of the beer (drink the rest) 1 tbsp. peanut butter

*Stir often and simmer on low heat 2-5 hours. Add
beer or water to thin, but not too much.
Garnish with chopped onion and cheddar cheese.
Serve with tortilla chips or corn bread.
Serves 8-10*

Curried Carrot & Rice

A wonderfully tasty and flavorful vegetarian dish.

Cook rice for about 25-30 minutes, until fluffy:	1/3 cup white rice 2/3 cup water
Reduce heat and add vegetable base and green curry paste:	2/3 tsp. vegetable base 2/3 tsp. green curry paste
In separate pot, cook carrots, bell peppers, ginger and sun-dried tomatoes until veggies are tender:	1 lg. carrot, diced 1/2 green bell pepper, diced 1/2 red bell pepper, diced 1/4 cup sun-dried tomatoes, chopped 1 tsp. minced ginger
In food processor, blend rice mixture & veggie mixture to make a smooth puree. Return to pot & add curry powder, salt, garlic, thyme, and coconut milk.	1 tsp. curry powder 2/3 tsp. granulated garlic 2/3 tsp salt Pinch of thyme 3/4 cup coconut milk

Heat to 160°.
Garnish with a sprig of parsley

34

Multi Veggie Chili

A delicious veggie-intensive meatless chili from a health-foods freak. It also makes a great salsa!

Spray nonstick dutch oven or large skillet with nonstick cooking spray. Heat over medium high heat until hot. Cook 5 minutes, stirring frequently.

1 cup chopped green bell peppers
1 cup chopped celery
1 cup chopped onion
3 cloves garlic, minced

Stir in, bring to a boil. Reduce heat, simmer uncovered 8-10 minutes or until celery is crisp-tender and flavors are blended, stirring occasionally:

1 (15 oz.) can tomato sauce
1 (15 1/2 oz.) can pinto beans, drained & rinsed
1 cup frozen whole kernel corn (or zucchini)
1 1/4 cups water
2 tsp. chili powder
1 tsp. dried oregano

Serves 4

Turkey Vatapa

*An unusual and different dish,
good enough to set before
the Queen (or King).*

Heat oil in pot over medium-high heat. Add onions, garlic and sauté:

1 tsp. olive oil
1/2 cup chopped onion
2 tsp. minced garlic

Add jalapenos and ginger and sauté. Add tomatoes, water and beer and bring to boil. Cover and reduce heat; let simmer for 20 minutes:

1 tbsp. fresh ginger, minced
1 jalapeno pepper, minced
1 cup water
1 (28 oz.) can diced tomatoes, undrained
1 (12 oz.) can light beer

Grind peanuts in food processor until finely chopped. Add to pot along with turkey and coconut milk:

1/4 cup dry unsalted peanuts
3 cups diced turkey
1/2 cup coconut milk

Turn up heat, simmer for 5 minutes. Stir in parsley, cilantro, lime juice, salt and pepper:

1/3 cup parsley, finely chopped
1/3 cup cilantro, finely chopped
1 tbsp. lime juice
1 tsp. salt
1 tsp. black pepper

*Garnish with cilantro or lime slices.
Serves 4-6.*

Greek Meat Sauce

Pickling spices and cinnamon provide an added touch to this aromatic sauce. It's good tossed with almost any Greek or Italian (or American) dish any time you want a meat sauce with the touch of the exotic.

In a wide frying pan, cook onions in butter, over medium high heat until onions are limp. Transfer to Dutch oven or 8-qt. pan:

6 large onions, finely chopped
4 tbsp. butter

In the frying pan, brown meat in 4 portions, adding butter as needed for each portion:

6 lbs. lean ground beef
4 tbsp. butter

Add meat to onions. Place garlic, cinnamon sticks and pickling spices in a cheese-cloth bag for easy removal:

3 cloves garlic, minced or pressed
2 sticks cinnamon
1 tbsp. whole mixed pickling spice

Add to meat and onion mixture along with tomato paste, salt, pepper to taste, and water:

6 (6 oz.) cans tomato paste
2 tbsp. salt
Freshly ground pepper
1 quart water

Cover and simmer, stirring occasionally, for 3 hours or until flavors are blended and sauce has thickened. Makes 4 quarts. Freeze in smaller portions to use as needed.

Eat what you want

The Japanese eat very little fat and suffer fewer heart attacks than the British or Americans.

On the other hand, the French eat a lot of fat and also suffer fewer heart attacks than the British or Americans.

The Japanese drink very little red wine and suffer fewer heart attacks than the British or Americans.

The Italians drink excessive amounts of red wine, and also suffer fewer heart attacks than the British or Americans

Conclusion: Eat and drink what you like. It's speaking English that kills you.

Broccoli Cheddar Pot Pie

*A rich and flavorful pot pie with a
Parmesan Biscuit Topping.*

Microwave on high until potatoes are soft; place into large bowl:	2 lg. potatoes cut in small cubes 1/2 cup butter 1 lg. onion, chopped 2 carrots, peeled & diced 3 celery stalks, sliced 1/4 cup sherry 2 tbsp. minced garlic
Microwave for 3 minutes, or until it can be blended together. Pour mixture over the vegetables.	3 cups milk 1 cup grated cheddar or processed cheese spread
Add to vegetable mixture and mix thoroughly.	50 oz. of canned cream of potato soup 1 cup cheddar cheese, shredded 3 cups chopped broccoli If using frozen, thaw first 1/4 tsp. white pepper 1/3 tbsp. garlic powder

*Scoop 1 1/2 cups of mixture into oven proof soup bowls.
Top with parmesan biscuit rounds (recipe on next page).
Brush with egg white. Bake at 350° for 20-25 minutes
until bubbly and golden brown. Makes 6 large pot pies.*

*For a Chicken Pot Pie, use 3 1/2 cups cooked, diced chicken for
broccoli, add 1/8 tsp. sage and 1/4 tsp. rosemary.*

Pot Pie Parmesan
Biscuit Topping

Yummy! Makes 6 large pot pie toppings.

Mix on low speed of mixer just until blended:	2 cups flour
	1 tbsp. baking powder
	1 tsp. sugar
	1/2 tsp. salt
	1/2 tsp. pepper
	1/2 tsp. paprika
	1/2 cup parmesan shredded
	2 tbsp. chopped green onions
Add butter pieces and mix until coarse.	1/3 cup unsalted butter cut into 1/2 inch pieces
Blend in milk:	3/4 cup milk

Turn out onto a floured board and knead until the dough is no longer too sticky to work with.
Roll out dough to 1/4" thick.
Cut dough with paring knife, tracing around top of an upside down soup bowl.
Place biscuit rounds on the filled bowls.
Brush tops with egg whites .
Bake at 350° for 20-25 minutes until pot pies are bubbly and golden brown.

Colophon Pie Crust

For use with recipes for quiche or fruit pies.
These tasty dishes are among the
Colophon customers' favorites!

Blend in food processor for 10 seconds—no more. Mixture should be a course meal:

1/2 lb. unsalted butter, cubed
2 1/2 cups white flour
1 tsp. salt
2 tsp. sugar

Add slowly to running food processor. Blend until mixture just holds together. No longer than 30 seconds.

1/4 to 1/2 cup ice water

Turn dough out onto pastry cloth. Divide in thirds and pat into disks. Do not overwork this dough! Wrap in parchment and refrigerate for at least one hour. Flour a pastry cloth and roll dough from the center to the edge, turning pastry cloth and adding flour as necessary. When fitting into pie pan, allow about 1 1/2" extra dough.

Makes 3 crusts.
Crusts may be frozen after fitting into pie pan if they are wrapped well.

Pesto Quiche

Traditional egg pie with an Italian touch.

In unbaked 9" pie shell, layer half the mozzarella, the pesto, the sun-dried tomatoes and the rest of the cheese:

1 pie shell
3/4 cup ready-made pesto
1/2 cup sun-dried tomatoes
2 cups shredded mozzarella

Blend together:

4 eggs
1 1/2 cups milk

Pour batter over top of tomato/cheese mixture.
Bake at 400° for 10 minutes, or until crust is lightly browned.
Reduce temperature to 300° and bake until quiche is set and knife comes out clean.

Quiche may be made out of almost anything! Simply fill a pie shell with three cups of ingredients—meats, cheeses, or vegetables—and then pour egg mixture over the top.

For added flavor on many quiches, add 1/4 tsp. dry hot mustard, and 1/4 tsp. cayenne pepper or a dash ground black pepper to the egg mixture.

Makes one Quiche

TexMex Haystack

This recipe comes from one of our customers.
Try it, you'll like it!

Mix together:	1 (16 oz.) can refried beans 1 can bean dip Garlic powder to taste 1/4 cup thick Picante sauce
Spread into 10x10 inch or 9x13 inch pan. Mash:	4 avocados with small amount of lemon juice 2 tbsp. guacamole mix
Spread over bean layer. Then spread over avocados:	1 pint sour cream
Have on hand to dice, then mix enough together to make a third layer:	Green onion Tomatoes Black olives Lettuce.

Top with grated mild cheese.
Serve with corn or flour tortilla chips.

To expand the dish, add another can refried beans, plus
a little more salsa. If you can't get ripe avocados,
use frozen guacamole.

"This is the dressing which I have made!" the emperor declared. "It shall be known as Caesar's"

From "The Idiots of March"
by Mama Colophon

Colophon Caesar Dressing

*Several Colophon Chefs contributed their
best home Caesars to this dressing.
We make it without eggs.*

In a shaker bottle add,
then shake to mix.
Refrigerate.

1/2 cup olive oil
5 cloves pressed or
   minced garlic
1 tbsp. lemon juice
2 tsp. Worchestershire
   Sauce
1 tsp. Dijon Mustard
Freshly ground pepper

Toss together in
a large bowl:

Lettuce
Grated parmesan cheese
Homemade croutons

*Shake well before pouring over salad!
Serve with french bread.*

*For variations on this, add shrimp, smoked
salmon or avocado to the salad!*

Honey Sesame Dressing

A great dressing with an oriental flair.

In food processor or blender combine:	1/4 cup chopped onion 1 tsp fresh chopped ginger root
Add:	2/3 cup honey (softened in microwave)
Mix in mixer:	2 cups safflower oil 1 cup cider vinegar
To mixer add:	1 tsp. soy sauce 1/2 tsp. salt 1 tsp. paprika 1/2 tsp. dry mustard powder
Add food processor mixture to oil and vinegar in mixer. Then add:	1/3 cup toasted sesame seeds

If you need to toast the seeds, spread on a cookie sheet and bake at 350° 20-25 minutes until light brown.
Mix all together and refrigerate.

Shake well before serving!

Fat-Free Italian Artichoke Dressing

*A "good" fat-free dressing is such an unusual thing,
that when "Gourmet Magazine" discovered we had
one, they wrote and requested our recipe!*

Chop in food processor: 1 cup artichoke hearts,
packed in water
and drained

In mixer add: 1/4 cup chopped onion
1/2 cup apple cider vinegar
1 cup water
1/2 cup apple juice
concentrate
1/4 cup minced garlic
1/8 cup honey
2 tsp. basil
2 tsp. oregano
1/2 tsp. white pepper

*Mix in artichoke hearts and refrigerate.
Shake well before serving!*

Although the tomato is botanically a fruit, the U. S. Supreme Court in 1893 ruled the tomato to be legally a vegetable because it is ". . . usually served at dinner, in, with, or after the soup, fish or meat, which constitutes the principal part of the repast, and not, like fruits, generally as a dessert."

Jack's Cornet Bay Salad

*This attractive but simple salad comes to us from
a man who loves cooking as much, or more,
than he loves the graphics business.*

Slice into six segments. Press segments gently to form a cup:	4 firm tomatoes
Chop fine: Mix vegetables with dressing and place in tomato cup.	1 cucumber 1/2 stalk celery 1/4 red pepper
Mix together for dressing:	1 cup mayonnaise Capful lemon juice 1/4 cup pickle juice 1 tbsp. sugar 1/4 cup catsup 1/4 cup relish

*Top with crab or shrimp.
Chill before serving.
Makes 4 servings.*

Spinach Salad

Recipe is from Catrina's Restaurant in Hayward, California.
We get around, don't we?

Clean, wash and dry the spinach. Chill well.	2 bunches spinach
Trim bacon of excess fat. Sauté the bacon over medium heat until soft, not crisp.	4 slices lean bacon
Add to bacon:	1 tbsp. Worchestershire Sauce 1 tbsp. Dijon style mustard 1/4 cup red wine vinegar 1/4 cup sugar

Stir and heat through.
Pour over spinach and toss well.
Serve with freshly ground pepper

Hummus

An exotic blend of healthy stuff that tastes great on bagels, as a vegetable dip, or on vegetarian sandwiches.

Purée in food processor for 3 to 4 minutes:	4 cups cooked, drained garbanzo beans 2 tsp. cumin 2 tsp. salt 1/2 cup minced garlic 1 cup olive oil
Add:	1 (15 oz.) can or jar of Tahini (ground sesame seeds) 1 3/4 cups lemon juice

Blend in food processor until thoroughly mixed, then refrigerate.

Makes approximately 4 cups of Hummus

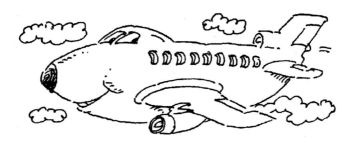

"Boss, de plane!" he cried, heading for
the landing strip and the
shipment of decadent desserts, which
surely must have arrived.

From "Fantasy Food Island"
by Mama Colophon

Desserts, etc.

*Desserts is just stressed
spelled backwards!*

Colophon Chocolate Chunk Cake

One of our most requested decadent dessert recipes, this one keeps them coming back!

Whisk together and set aside:	2/3 cup cocoa 1 cup boiling water
Cream together, then add the cocoa mixture:	3/4 cup butter 1 1/4 cup brown sugar 2/3 cup white sugar 2 eggs 1 egg yolk 1 tbsp. vanilla
Blend together and mix on high speed for 30 seconds:	3 cups white flour 1/2 tsp. salt 2 tsp. baking soda
Add slowly, mix on medium speed, scraping bowl often, for 30 seconds:	1 2/3 cups buttermilk

Pour batter into greased and floured 10 in. cake pan and bake at 350° until knife inserted comes out clean. Cook thoroughly and frost with Chocolate Frosting.

Makes one layer cake

Colophon Chocolate Frosting

*Very rich, creamy frosting for Chocolate Chunk Cake
or any other homemade goodies.*

Cream together: 1 cup soft butter
    1 1/2 cups cocoa powder

Add and mix well: 3 1/2 cups powdered sugar

Add very slowly to mixer: 1/2 cup Half & Half

*Mix all together on high for 15 seconds, scraping bowl
thoroughly.*

*Frost cake and garnish top with whole milk
chocolate chips or grated chocolate
and nuts if desired.*

Frosts one layer cake

Colophon Peanut Butter Pie

This pie is so delicious, "Bon Appetit" requested our recipe and printed it in the August, 1993 issue. This recipe is a 2 pager, and makes 2 pies.

Mix together in a large bowl and set aside:
- 1 (8 oz.) cream cheese
- 1 1/2 cups crunchy peanut butter
- 1 1/2 cups brown sugar
- 1 tsp. vanilla

Whip on low speed for two minutes:
- 2 cups heavy whipping cream

Add and whip on high speed until peaks form (do NOT overwhip or cream will turn buttery!):
- 1/2 cup powdered sugar

Fold the whipped cream mixture into the peanut butter mixture.
Divide mixture into two 8 inch Chocolate Cookie Crusts.
Spread evenly and freeze pies for 3 hours.
(Recipe continued on next page.)

Colophon Peanut Butter Pie
Continued
And the cookie crust to bake them in!

Melt in separate bowl in the microwave for 30-45 seconds. Stir until smooth

2 cups melting chocolate (or semisweet chocolate chips)
1/2 cup Half & Half

Pie topping: Carefully spoon half the chocolate ganache on the top of each frozen pie. Spread evenly and quickly garnish with 1 tbsp. chopped peanuts before the chocolate sets. Chill for 1 hour before cutting. Use a knife dipped in hot water for cutting.

This recipe makes two pies.
They may be frozen for storage.
To thaw, place in refrigerator for several hours.
They will cut more easily if partially frozen.

Chocolate Cookie Crust
For the Colophon Peanut Butter Pie

Combine well by hand or food processor
4 1/2 cups finely ground chocolate cookie crumbs
and 1/2 cup butter melted
Divide in half and press into two pie tins.
Bake 7-10 minutes at 350°

Cookies!

Wonder just who fashioned the first cookie,
and under what circumstance.
Perhaps some stone-age mother robbed a bee's
nest for honey, spread it on a leftover piece of
dough made from stone-ground wheat or
barley, and baked it over the flowing coals of
the morning fire after the family
had finished off breakfast.
Back then it was "waste not, want not,"
much as it should continue to be.
And lo! The cookie was born!

Dave's Breakfast Cookies

*Low-Fat cookies make great tasting
healthful snacks.*

Mix together in
mixing bowl:
1 1/2 cups applesauce
1 1/8 cups brown sugar
1/2 cup apple juice
1/6 cup orange juice
1/6 cup lemon juice
2 tbsp. vanilla

Mix in:
1 mashed banana

Stir in:
3/4 cup flour
1/2 cup wheat flour
1 tbsp. baking soda
1/2 tbsp. cinnamon
1/2 tbsp. nutmeg
1/2 tbsp. ginger
3/4 tsp. cloves

Stir in:
4 cups oats
2 cups Rice Krispies
3/4 cup crushed cornflakes
3/4 cups dried fruit

*These cookies are very moist. It is easiest to use an ice
cream scoop and drop the dough on a parchment lined
cookies sheet. Dip fingers into water and pat cookies
into flat circles. Bake at 325° 12-15 minutes. They will
not spread while baking. Makes 24 cookies*

Colophon Cookies

Good :)

One of our hottest selling cookies.

Cream together:	1 cup butter
	1 cup brown sugar
	1/2 cup white sugar
Add and mix:	2 eggs
	1/2 tbsp. vanilla
Add:	2 cups white flour
	1 tsp. baking powder
	1 tsp. baking soda
	1/2 tsp. salt
Add:	1 3/4 cups oats
	1 1/2 cups Rice Krispies
	3/4 cup white choc chips
	3/4 cup butterscotch chips
	3/4 cup pecans

Drop batter onto nonstick cookie sheet.
Bake at 350" until golden
Makes 20 medium or 10 giant cookies

Hey diddle diddle
I've a bulge in my middle
I hope to whittle it soon.
But eating's such fun,
I won't get it done,
'Til my dish runs away
   with my spoon! *D. Neil*

Bapple Cookies

Like "trail mix" in a cookie, many people eat just these instead of a full lunch!

Cream together in a large bowl:	3/4 cup butter
	3/4 cup white sugar
	1/2 cup brown sugar
	3 eggs, add one at a time
Add:	3/4 tsp. vanilla
	1/2 cup apple juice
	1/8 cup cooled espresso
Mix together:	2 1/2 cups flour
	2 tsp. baking soda
	1/2 tsp. salt
	1/2 tsp. allspice
	1/2 tsp. nutmeg
	2 tsp. cinnamon
	3 3/4 cups oats
Stir in and mix well, scraping sides and bottom of bowl:	1 med. chopped apple
	3/4 cup raisins
	3/4 cup chocolate chips
	1/2 cup chopped walnuts

Drop rounded spoonfuls of dough onto parchment lined cookie sheet. Dip fingers in cold water and press cookies into round, flat patties. They will not spread. Sprinkle each with 1/2 tsp. chopped walnuts. Bake at 325° 10-12 min. or until light to med brown. Do not overcook! Makes about 2 dozen large cookies

A Fat Cat

A cat is good for catching mice,
A horse is good for hauling,
A pig is good to roast and slice,
A calf is good for bawling.

A frog has most expensive legs,
A ram is good for mutton,
A hen is good for laying eggs,
A squirrel is good for nuttin'!

Low Fat Muffins

Health Clubs buy these from us.
They taste too good to be low fat!

Mix on high speed for one minute to break up whites:	1 cup sugar 5 egg whites
Add and mix:	2 teaspoons vanilla 3/4 cup applesauce 1/2 cup nonfat sour cream 1 cup buttermilk
Combine and add to wet mixture. Do not overmix!	3 3/4 cup white flour 1 1/2 tbsp. baking powder 1 tsp. baking soda 1/2 tsp. salt
Stir into flour mixture:	1 cup fresh or frozen fruit

Fill paper muffin cups.
Sprinkle lightly with sugar.
Bake at 325° for 15 minutes or until
pick comes out clean.

Makes 8 large muffins

Good ☺
Janine loves

Peanut Butter Fantasies

Decadently special dessert bars.
Wonderful!

Cream together:
3/4 cup butter
3/4 cup brown sugar
1 egg
1/2 tsp. vanilla

Add and mix:
3/4 cup wheat flour
3/4 cup white flour
1/2 tsp. baking powder
1/4 tsp. baking soda
1/4 tsp. salt

Press mixture. Bake at 325° for 15 minutes, or until crust is lightly browned:
Dip fingers in water and press mixture into greased and floured 9X13 inch pan.

Cream together and spread over top of crust:
1/2 cup butter
2 cups crunchy peanut butter
1/2 teaspoon vanilla
1 cup powdered sugar

Sprinkle on top of peanut butter:
1 1/2 cups semisweet chocolate chips

Bake pan in 325° oven for 1 to 2 minutes to melt chocolate.
Garnish with toasted coconut. Chill before cutting.

The Yogi's Banana Bread

*Discovered in the 70's
by a Yogi in Bellingham.*

Mix in food processor:

1 cup brown sugar
1/2 cup softened butter
2 eggs
3 or 4 very ripe bananas

Add to food processor
and blend thoroughly:

2 cups flour
1 tsp. baking powder
1/2 tsp. salt
1/2 tsp. baking soda
1 tsp. cinnamon
1 tsp. cloves
1 tsp. nutmeg

Add to food processor
and blend very lightly:

1 cup frozen blueberries
1 cup chopped cashews

*Bake in well greased loaf pan at 325° for
about 1 hour. Test with a knife to see if it's
done in the middle. Remove from pan and set
on wire rack to cool.
Slice and serve.*

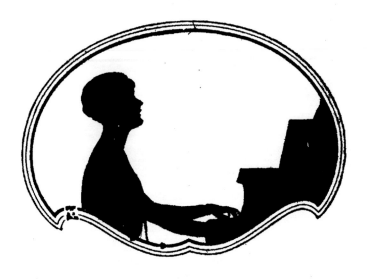

Marge Starks, the creator of "Old Marge's Cheesecake," is a great musician and a great human being. A Seattle pianist, Marge has released several recordings of her standards, and show tunes from the 1930s to now, to benefit "Rosehedge," an assisted living residence for AIDS patients in Seattle.

Old Marge's Cheesecake

Marge's son Jim taught us how to make this divinely rich cheesecake while we were in college. He once sold them to restaurants in Cannon Beach, Oregon.

Mix in food processor and press mixture into bottom of glass pie pan to form a crust. Bake crust 10 minutes at 375°:

1 pkg. (1/4 lb.) graham crackers, crushed
3/4 melted stick of butter
1/4 cup sugar

In mixer, blend until smooth & pour into crust. Bake again for 20 minutes:

2 (8 oz.) packages softened cream cheese
2 eggs
1/2 cup sugar
1 tsp. vanilla

Mix by hand:

1 cup sour cream
1/2 tsp. vanilla
1/2 tsp lemon juice
2 tbsp. sugar

Pour mixture over pie and smooth with knife or spatula. Bake again for five minutes. Remove from oven, cool and refrigerate. Serve very cold as is, or with berries on top.

Makes one pie.

Apple Crisp

A dessert that combines basic apple and oatmeal goodness is sure to be loved by all. Sweet enough for the young, it also complements an after-dinner cup of coffee.

Spread thinly sliced apples over the bottom of a greased 8x8x2-inch baking dish.

4 or 5 medium-size tart cooking apples, cored peeled, & sliced thinly

In a mixing bowl, combine the brown sugar, granulated sugar, flour and oats, then stir in the melted butter:

6 tbsp. firmly packed light brown sugar
6 tbsp. granulated sugar
1/2 cup unsifted all-purpose flour
3/4 cup uncooked quick-cooking rolled oats
1/2 cup (1 stick) butter, melted

Spread mixture over the apples. Pour the water evenly over the top.

1/2 cup water

Bake, uncovered, in 375° preheated oven, until apples are tender, about 30 minutes. Serve warm or at room temperature with whipped cream or ice cream, if desired. Serves 4.

Almond-Vanilla Apples

This recipe is a bit unusual, and comes to us from that other coast, even though it uses our wonderful Washington apples.

Peel, core & thinly slice apples. Toss with lemon juice to coat. Butter a 1 1/2 qt. baking dish and spread apples over the bottom:

- 2 1/2 lbs. tart cooking apples
- 1 1/2 tbsp. fresh lemon juice

Sift together flour, sugar, salt and cinnamon. Stir in almonds:

- 1 cup sifted flour
- 1 1/2 cups sugar
- 1/4 tsp. salt
- 1/4 tsp. cinnamon
- 2/3 cup almonds, finely chopped

Mix the melted butter with the vanilla:

- 1/2 cup unsalted butter, melted
- 1 tsp. vanilla extract

Add almond-flour mixture and toss with fork until mixed and crumbly. Sprinkle evenly over apples. Bake at 375° un til topping is richly browned, about 35-40 minutes. Can be made ahead. Serve with softly whipped cream. Serves 6.

Colophon's Best Recipes
Alphabetical Index

A BIG THANK YOU to all Colophon staff, past and present, who contributed their culinary knowledge and special recipes to the Colophon Cafe. Thanks also to our many customers around the world, whose thoughtful comments and appreciative palates made this book possible.

MAMA COLOPHON
(our founder)

Notes

_____
_____
_____
_____
_____
_____
_____
_____
_____
_____
_____
_____
_____
_____
_____
_____
_____
_____
_____
_____
_____
_____
_____

ISLAND IMAGES, INC.
OAK HARBOR, WASHINGTON
An Island Images Publication